THE ILLUMINAUTICAL:

THE ILLUMINAUTICAL:

Musings of the Rum Poet

ROBERT B. SHEFF

ISBN-13: 9781540732934
ISBN-10: 1540732932

Thank you for giving me this opportunity to introduce you to not only my work but also to myself. I've always enjoyed writing—whether a poem for a friend or just some words I'd like to express.

I've learned that in order to write, you must write what you know. It took many years (and sometimes I'm still not sure), but I gathered my nine years spent in the US Navy, my love of history, and my creative bone to conjure a few rhymes here and there.

I grew up in Charleston, West Virginia, always knowing that I would spend time serving my country in the US Navy. I knew this ever since learning of my father's service during World War II. I knew then I too would serve. And as a Radioman for nine years I did!

I met some of the most wonderful people from all around America from different backgrounds and nationalities, and they have certainly enriched my life! *Thank you*, shipmates!

The following pages are broken down into self-explanatory chapters. I hope that within these pages, you find something that touches your heart, your soul, and/or your funny bone, or maybe just gives you cause to reflect.

Thank you.

Intrepidly yours,
Robert B. Sheff (*a.k.a., The Rum Poet*)

ACKNOWLEDGMENTS

This collection of rhymes would not be possible without the following places and people who allowed me inspiration to create and/or to just sit and write. So, thank you to the following Bars and Restaurants:

The Tricky Fish, the Empty Glass, Yen's Sandwiches, Red Carpet, Main Kwong, and Moxxee Coffee. And thank you to these friends and loved ones for providing me with love, inspiration, nourishment, and smiles: Greg Rosencrance, Jim Smallridge, Gary Sheff, Jane Charnock, Mattie Rae Soles, Debbie Kanner Ebner, Ivor Sheff, Newman Jackson, Pam Snodgrass Hylbert Eder, Jo Burka, Carolyn Faber, Russell Young, Dennis Hedrick, Kathy Smith, Marcy Robinson Myers, Misti Hayes Assaley, Ann Charnock, Salli Allison, Al Nelson, Earl Barnes, Kency Coes, Mike Vanjelgerhuis, Mike Kingston, Wayne Soehrmann, Chris Douthit, Agnes Rhee Ahn, Andy Richardson, Barbie Dallman, Carrie and Mike Stalnaker, Rich Boyle, Ron King, Jay Myers, Marilyn and Victor Urecki, Marie Shelton, Margie Alderson, Illene Goodman, Jim Lange, Laura and Richard Fenton, Mark Scoular, David L. Williams, Ric Cochran, Jim Snyder, Julie and Richard Zegeer, Robin and Brenda Wilson, Florence Sheff, Mom, Dad, and my brother, Arthur.

Special thank you to Patricia Chirino for your beautiful cover artwork! And Thank You Jim Lange for my "Rum Poet" moniker. Jim and I have a deep affection for the beverage, also in tandem with the rhymes I'd post on social media, he dubbed me, *"The Rum Poet."*

But I save the best for last—thank you to a lady whom I consider my sister-in-law, Jackie Loizou Rosencrance. It was you who told me, "Get all your poems together and send them to me!" Had it not been for you, these poems would still be scattered throughout my domicile, my computer, and in my iPhone. So, with love in my heart, I say, "Thank you so very much!"

CONTENTS

I. THOUGHTFUL VERSE

LET LOVE BE

Loving the earth and all that she brings...
The smiles on faces of wonderful things
The flowers, the animals, the grass, and the woods
To all loving beings with this understood

The beautiful smiles shine out to all
All comes around, for all those who call
Breathe in the joy and exhale without—
Share all the wonder, give it a shout!

Feel only love, all you can do...
Feel all the love, from me—to you
Love all you see, love you and love me
Love all around, feel it and be!

POSITIVE THOUGHTS

Looking for your passion
To feeling great all day,
Think and know that what you believe
Will soon be on its way

Think a joyous feel…
And project a little smile,
Feel it from the top of your head
And know it'll be worthwhile

All the outside drama…
That's merely earthly bound…
What you are is so much more
Just *be* what you have found!

All those negative thoughts
Wash right down the drain…
Just sing and smile with all your soul
And dance out in the rain!

JUST BE

Skies of wonder
Seas of dreams
Deepest depths
To highest extremes

In between
And outside in
Inside out
And from within

All around
And side to side
Once closed off
Now open wide

Truth unfurled
Wrong now right
Euphoria found
Dwell in the light

SORROW REVEALED

(Inspired by a painting titled *Sorrow Revealed* by the artist
Newman Jackson)

Sorrow revealed, a heavenly sight
The past that was dark, gave into light

Sorrow revealed, a mournful gaze
A search ahead, for happier days

Sorrow revealed, a goodbye wave
Take a deep breath it's time to be brave

Sorrow revealed, up from above
Set deep within, and nestled in love

LIVE YOUR LIFE IN LOVE

If you live your life in fear
You'll lose all that you hold dear
Your friends, your family
Your drive, your life
You're sure to never see clear…

But if you live your life in love
You'll feel all that you're proud of
Just let it shine from your face
With a smile to showcase
From within, and without
And above.

SOMETHING GOOD IS HAPPENING

Innate knowledge deep within
Time awaits...to share again

Whispering celestial spirits explain
But are hidden inside this Earthly plane

Introspect and thoughtful meditation
Hope for purpose and revelation

Still derived and still encrypted
Yet continue on the veil unscripted

Different vernacular
Result spectacular

Sentient being particular

The incomprehensible becomes awake
My entire form starts to shake!

Languorous return to my celestial origin
Into the cosmos until restored again

Something good is happening
Something good is happening

RECIPE FOR EARTH

The North Star, or Polaris
Earth's ancient navigation
Plotted on this steady course
Leads to emancipation

These shackles called gravity
Which tether me to Earth
Living a human existence taught
We're less than we are worth

To only know our magnificence
We soon could rise above
The earthly greed and ignorance
Release it all and love!

THE ARTISTS

Musicians and poets
The artist who paints
Serve up their talents
To sinners and saints

Music and lyric
To dance and to sing
Sweetest of sounds
Their ambience rings

Colors are painted
That pleasures the eye
Bathed in the light
Or a subtle imply

Ah, but the verse
Impassioned within
Reaching so deeply
From where it has been

Rolled into one
Set free as a dove
To fill in our hearts
The importance of love

Touching one's soul
From within to without
Lighting the way
What life's all about

This is the gift
The three have to give
Giving life all its passion
The way we should live

LIGHTED MOON

Lighted moon shining bright
Reflecting suns firelight
Gaze upon its shining hue
Consuming star bright silver blue

Imposing girth and subtle force
A gravitational stirring source
An influential lunar trance
Inciting wonder and romance

SHAMEFUL THINGS

Shameful things that I have done
Of which I'm not so proud
I want to teach of my bad deeds
I want it told out loud

But then again, since *karma* knows
And knows I feel ashamed
Maybe *karma* will understand
And I won't be badly blamed

But yes, I know the only way
To fix whatever's done
Is fix the wrong that is my fate
And cool my smoking gun

Sincerely speak the honest truth
With reason and with courage
Accept the fate and do what's right
And hope to have advantage

IN THE NOW

As we glance around not taking time
To hear and see without...
We miss the things important for us
To laugh and sing about...

But if we listen, really, really listen
To what the soul says from within...
And live our life set in the now
Instead of where it's been

RAIN

The din of rain upon my windowpane
No sunshine today, to my disdain

If the light outside is dreary and drawn
And no relief by the breaking dawn

Close your eyes and seek what's sought
Of what will be, by mindful thought

Brought from within, spread light outside
And light will reign both far and wide

When all you have is in array
No outside force will rue the day!

ENOUGH!

It's time to clear the energy
Declutter all this space
Smash it, trash it, or stash it
Then exit this rat race

Away with cluttered memories
Away with what's dogmatic
Gather up imagined beliefs
And those toys up in the attic

Say goodbye and fare-thee-well
Unfasten curtains drawn
All that was is now no more
Adieu! To all that's gone

Look inside within yourself
The answers are within
Refresh, restart, begin anew
Ahead from where you've been

Awakened spirit recognized
Arise— frec as a dove
What once was cloaked is realized—
Imparting gracious love

THE RHYMING POEM

Most poems today
They don't care to rhyme...
They are free to explore—
And twist around time

But remember the days
Of alliteration
With that rhythm and beat
That divine syncopation

You'd savor the word...
You feel it's your duty
When reading Lord Byron's...
"She Walks in Beauty"

Or "Do not go gentle
into that Good Night"
Are words Dylan Thomas
Set down to write

"O Captain! My Captain"
A Walt Whitman tutorial...
To Abraham Lincoln
A President's Memorial

If you found a "Brown Penny"
And enjoy all its traits...
You know whom to thank
William B. Yeats

And if flowers adorn
All good that's on Earth…
"Daffodils" are the choice
By William Wordsworth

Then Robert Frost
Just send him a greeting…
"Stopping by Woods
on a Snowy Evening"

Then if some dark night
Outside your chateau
You hear quoth "The Raven"
By Edgar A. Poe

Oh, so many
With rhyme to enjoy…
But I still remember
When I was a boy…

Ah, my favorite
As a young little brat…
The crowd and I'd cheer with
"Casey at the Bat"

THE EARTHLY FEAR OF LOVE

(Partially inspired by the song "A World Without Love" by Peter and Gordon, and the book of the same name, by Dallas Doctor)

Being alone too long
Creates thoughts of inadequacy
Your every gift is flawed
Your each and every flaw
Becomes hideous

You are shameful…and you believe it
And you know it. So, you hide

You hide behind masks and deeds
Masks of smiles and laughter, deeds of daily
Compositions that return you to your room
Of painful comfort. Your room of empty space
Your painful room of loneliness and despair

This pain is familiar. This pain you know
It is your only trusted friends. You know that it will never
Leave you. It remains your constant companion.
Growing roots inside your heart to protect you from any
Penetration of change

But there may be change. There can be change
Change from outside your room of protection. You are
Warned to be aware of the outside forces. Beware of change

Change will cast you to the unknown. The unknown that is
Unseeable, unpredictable, unfamiliar, and yes, unbearable
Change. Change takes courage. It takes strength. Strength
Instilled by the outside force. That force of which you were
Warned. Fear it. Fear the change. Until...your courage is
Fueled. Fueled by the outside force. And now it
Becomes too late. Change is evident. Change is imminent
The change, the outside force...are love

You no longer remain alone.

FORGIVENESS

I take this chance to move up and beyond
Replacing burden with melodious lightness…
Deprived your admission
I still offer submission
And bestow you my forgiveness

I float above with only love
Emancipated and weightless…
My captive thoughts no longer tethered
I'm freed with my forgiveness

(Inspired by a song of the same name, written by Jim Lange. Thanks Jim!)

2. SEASONS AND SPORTS

MEMORIAL DAY

To those veterans who served
But now have passed,
We remember your strength
And courage, steadfast

The bugle sounds
Taps is rendered,
Your honorable service
Has never surrendered

Peace and thanks
We graciously send,
And salute you all
This Memorial Weekend

SUMMER BEACHIN'

Summer is here, time to set me free
There's only one place that I want to be
With a beach umbrella and my toes in the sand
Where the string bikinis my eyes will land

Warmest of breezes brushes my skin
Radio playin' a tropical din
Beverage is cool, right by my side
Numbing my senses, as I imbibe

NOT...CASEY AT THE BAT

(Or "Joe, Where Are Ye?")

The outlook wasn't brilliant for the Bombers from the Bronx...
With "Blow-Hard" Jr., at the helm and the cellar—they ensconce

Rodriguez again, as so before—his bat failed to produce...
The crowd reacts: "A-Rod, you bum" So quickly they deduce

They thought the former catcher, "Joe," would make a final dash,
But Giambi's making 23 mil, and cares more about his 'stache

Damon's out in center, where another Joe once roamed—
And he lied to his ol' Boston fans and from their lips they still foam

Even with the millions paid————victory's just a canard—
This year they could not win their league,or clinch a wild card!

If only they were paid much more, their bats would find their groove—
And maybe their stadium wouldn't be torn down, and they wouldn't have
to move!

Oh, somewhere in this favored land it's a bright and sunny day
But *not* here in this East Coast Borough—for Joe Torre's in LA!

2011

For the Yankees, it's been quite a year…
Questions of Posadas and Jeter's career,
And to New York and Girardi
The Tigers staved off their party—
And gave Yank fans a rousing Bronx cheer

YANKEES SCALPED BY INDIANS

The Yankees again lost their glory
But that is not—the end of this story
'Cause with a little perspiration
The Indians gave swift scalpitation
And the "boss" will now fire Joe Torre

MEET THE METS

Meet the Mets they'll cover your bets
Just be sure and keep all your stubs…
Because you'll lose all your cash
While those with panache
Have bet on the Chicago Cubs!

Go Cubs!

A BASEBALL POEM

As autumn permeates the soul
Of Major League Baseball...
I can't put off this forlorn feeling
Of what will follow fall

The leaves will turn brown and gold
And a chill will fill the air
For at the end of the Fall Classic
Fans' thoughts turn to despair

Of course, we have college football
And the exciting NFL...
But nothing seems to warm the soul
Where bleacher bums would dwell

We endure the winter months
Like a hibernating bear
We drive around our baseball park
But know there's nothing there

We watch a classic movie,
Bull Durham or *Field of Dreams*...
We read about "Mighty Casey"
Where no joy in Mudville deems

We pass the time as best we can
In a dilatory state
Until spring training comes in March
Till then we just can't wait

That's when we wake from slumber
And dust-off bat and glove
Our time of year is finally here
And to the game we love

CINCO DE MAYO

Happy Cinco de Mayo!
A battle won south of the Bayo'
The French took a beating
So, we drink while we're eating
And now everyone knows why-o!

SPRINGTIME POEM

New beginnings, is what springtime brings,
The sun will shine and the birds will sing!

Anew! Anew! A fresh start begins,
Filled with songs and sweet violins

Spread your wings and prepare to soar,
Forget whatever was - open, any closed door

Embrace opportunities with class and with style,
And open yourself, to all with a smile

SUMMER

Summer is here time to set me free
There's only one place that I want to be
With a beach umbrella and my toes buried deep in the sand
Where the string bikinis will cover whatever's not tanned

SUMMER SOLSTICE

Summer Solstice has arrived
The longest day of the year
The sun appears to stand so still
In the northern hemisphere

Reaching its northerly point
Above the Tropic of Cancer
Twenty-three and a half degrees—axial tilt
If you're looking for an answer

First day of summer, sun, and warmth
The grass is soft and green
Restless people rise about
All over to be seen

Breathe it in and breath it out
No more looking for a sign
Answers are all found within
Enhanced by warm sunshine

ANOTHER BASEBALL POEM

Warmer weather turning cold
Dwindling, the boys of summer
Playoff time turns leaves to gold…
And to some—that is a bummer

No more sunny bleacher days—
With players in long sleeves…
They try to fend off autumn's chill
And October nighttime freeze

Some make do with football games
Or winterize their homes…
Some will think of holidays
And break out those stupid gnomes

But me I say enjoy the rest—
Of what baseball has to give
Still green grass and boyhood dreams—
Those guys know how to live!

If your team is still alive
Or still has many queries…
Enjoy the boys just one more time
"From playoffs—through World Series."

After that, the baseball fans
Will stow their bat and glove…
They'll say goodbye to bleacher friends
And to the game they love…

They'll bundle up for winter months—
All the while, restraining...
Till someone finally says, "Play ball!"
And commencement of spring training!

SUMMER EVENING

Fresh-cut grass while the sun's still up
A lawn mower engine whines,
Porch-sitting weather with beverage in hand
Spring displays its signs

A neighbor's dog barks, while trees are still bare
As birds' flutter all around,
Still a chill in the air but without any despair
And I'll go pour me another round

A robin surveys my front lawn
As a squirrel darts here and there
Skies are blue as the sun sets course
As I still sit in my chair

A ball is bouncing and spices are free
A cookout is somewhere nearby
Shadows they're falling and I am recalling
If a third round is what I should try—

The breeze is wafting its' still chilly state
And I'm wondering how long I can last
Until spices and breeze bring me to my knees
And relentlessly break out a shot glass

AUTUMNAL EQUINOX

Earth's autumnal equinox—
The day and night now equal...
Last year's winter weather gone
Yet bringing forth a sequel

Bid adieu to summer sun
This message to forewarn
The sun displays a southern course
To the Tropic of Capricorn

As Earth's rotation oscillates
Lifting its equator
Twenty-three and a half degrees
The nights become much greater

Autumn glows its warmest hues
In our northern hemisphere
Yellow, red, and golden brown
Sweet colors to revere

Warmest breezes turn to chill
Without that much transgressing
Reminding us to take up stock
And count up all our blessings

HALLOWEEN'S GHOSTS AND GOBLINS

As the stars appear and the moonlight glows
The wind sends chills from your head to your toes

Ghosts and goblins, vampires and witches
A ghastly ghoul in bloody stitches

They turn out to bestow *cantankerous* intent
While witches fly by and the specters ascent

Down from the valleys, out through the street
Inside the alleys—together they meet

They'll creep up your steps, they'll rap on your door
They'll howl "Tricks or Treats" in hope of a score!

Please to appease these creatures when seen
And wish them and you—Happy Halloween!

HALLOWEEN

Roses are reddish
Pine trees are green
I hope everyone has—
"A Creepy Halloween!"

But should you decide
Yes, just in case—
You step outside
With a mask on your face

Do beware
Aside from the fun
If behind someone's mask
There really is none!

Run for your lives!
If you're not really sure
Or like that quote from the Raven,
Quoth, "Never more!"

HAPPY DIA DE LOS MUERTOS

Dia de los Muertos
The day of the dead!
They don't rise to scare
But party with us instead!

We dance with our ancestors
Whom we haven't seen in years
They open our eyes
That there's nothing to fear!

We're here for a while
Though it seems inconvenient
Not for us to break
Just bend very lenient

Our lessons we learn
They're not to chagrin…
But to see what once was
Or just what may have been

Not all written in stone…
Perchance for us to vary
Of what lies within
Or without us to tarry

So, on this day,
The Day of the Dead
Lift up terrestrial guise
And party with them instead!

TWAS THE NIGHT OF THE ORANGE BOWL

Twas the night of the Orange Bowl and throughout the nation
We were the underdogs on every TV and Radio Station
ESPN said we couldn't win - Clemson would destroy us in the end
Said our guys weren't so great, but one didn't know WV was a state!
The fans were nestled all snug in the stands
Clapping along with the Mountaineer band
And ma in her jammies and I in my WVU cap settled in for the game
A bowl of chips in my lap

When out on the field there arose such a clatter
I turned up the sound to see what was the matter
Touchdown after touchdown after
Touchdown they scored
Ten in all for a seventy score
The quarterback in charge was so lively and quick
I knew in a moment it was Geno Smith
More rapid than eagles his passes they came
Then he pointed and scrambled and called them by name

Now Austin! Now Bailey! Buie and Alston!
On Cook! On Brown! On Milhouse and Irvin!
Tightrope the side lines and reach for that score
We make history tonight, no one's done it before!

The coach praised his players, the fans stayed for hours
Dana still wet from his Gatorade shower
He turned with a jerk, to his team gave a whistle
And away they all flew like the down of a thistle
But I heard him exclaim, as he strode out of sight
'The couches are burning in Mo-town tonight!"

RIP ERNIE BANKS

Friday night in January
College football now is over…
Baseball season's far away
And then sad news, moreover…

Mr. Cub, Ernie Banks
"Let's play two" was his claim
With class and style now playing ball
In heaven's hall of fame

SCRAPING WINDOWS

(Inspired by Van Morrison's "Cleaning Windows")

Farthest north, south of the Mason-Dixon
Temperatures hover near zero
Where deepest south meets arctic weather
I'm stuck here scraping windows

I inhale the air as others do
And long for summer days
Where spring and autumn had once appeared
But I'm stuck here scraping windows

The chilly air casts despair
Without the warmth of youth
The long-ago ways of perfect days
While I'm stuck here scraping windows

The hazy gray of winter's day
And frozen pipes of ice
Wait for days of solar glaze
While I'm stuck here scraping windows

Moving south was once a myth
From my beloved family hearth
Not so much a bad idea
As I'm still here scraping windows

THANKSGIVING

The weather, it seems to be somewhat murky
While behind closed doors we dine on turkey

Watch football and eat—for some that's the plan
Or give in to naps, caused by tryptophan

Any way you slice it, with gravy and stuffing—
I wish all of you—a happy Thanksgiving!

If you're not feeling perky
By dining on turkey
And consuming too much tryptophan…
Just turn on football
And sleep through it all
'Cause that's always been *my* game plan!

HOLIDAY CHEER!

I just received a blessing
I know that's how you meant it
Although it's deemed politically incorrect
It's how I chose to accept it

"Merry Christmas" the blessing said…
Seems I hear it this time each year…
Though a Christian that I may not be
I'll revel with you in cheer!

Ya' see, I do not like to be accused
Un–-American, ungodly and unjust…
Because I know what we all should know
Our G-d loves all of us!

You must admit that all of us
Have had it crammed right down our throat—
"What's right is right and because I'm right
Let anyone else be smote!"

I know, I know…I know your point
Some brethren won't always accept it
But please know, please that I…
That I, know how you meant it

So please don't show me written text
Of what earthly man's hand has printed
Look inside *your soul* you'll find
What the Good Lord has imprinted

What's right, what's wrong, it's all inside
Just feel with deep reflection...
For, *loving all* is all needs said
And to deliver one another's affection!

(Do not allow religion to cause divisive behavior)

JEWISH HOLIDAYS

On Yom Kippur Eve
All we can conceive
Is when there'll be food in our belly
But then we'll sing "Hava Nagila"
Drink mas tequila
And maybe send out for some deli!

Throughout this year
May you find
A hand to help
If you're in a bind
And should someone near
Become distressed
May they then turn to you
And you *both* be blessed!
L'Shana Tova…
To you all
Inscribed this year
To have a ball!

It's time again to wish you all a happy healthy year—
To all my friends whom I love and certainly hold so dear
I wish you smiles that last for miles as you travel many roads,
And hold the hands of the ones you love, which help you share your load

NEW YEAR'S POEMS

If "New Year's wish" is said to you,
Please don't take it quite so lightly...
For in that wish a gift is sent
"Your start should shine so brightly!"

So, when you hear that wish this year,
Remember what you read...
And turn that wish right back on them
And hope your light will spread!

Another New Year, a chance for us to be among our friends
To health and wealth and happiness, here's hoping it never ends

We've endured joys and sorrows, but from it all arose
Our look upon our lives, gives a chance for us to compose...

A fresh and new existence, from within and without...
We can smile deep inside and hold it—then let it scatter about

Impose onto others, a caring—a caring, thoughtful gaze
Wish upon them peacefulness through in, throughout their days

And if this New Year you find yourself with a dreary little thought...
Remember that smile you have inside- it's time to break it out!

WINTER SOLSTICE

Winter solstice has arrived
The shortest day of the year
The season's begun, adieu
Mr. Sun—
From the Northern
Hemisphere

Reaching its southern most point
. With a message to forewarn...
Twenty-three and a half degrees
Above the Tropic of Capricorn

First day of winter, the wind and the cold
The leaves are gone from the trees
The longest night, absence of light
Forsaking any warm guarantees

VALENTINE

My dearest Valentine
I dreamt of you today...
I sat alone inside my thoughts
And dreamed my day away

As I dwelled upon your charm
I willed a mindful thought...
For when I dream throughout the day
It's you that I have sought

So, if you wonder where I am
Or if I might forget...
Just know that I am coming soon—
We just simply haven't met

PRELUDE TO VALENTINE'S

Prelude to Valentines
And give my attention
To a name to be nameless...
No honorable mention

Just a wish—
Without subtle clue...
Of whom is intended
Brought forward to you

Please take heart no need to align
But if alone—*be* your own—
Happy Valentine!

3. MINDFUL INTROSPECTION AND THE FAIRER SEX

MY MEMORY

Am I in love with you
Or is it just the memory of you,
Did we laugh that much?
Or is it just a memory

My memory is pretty funny
It turns my past to perfection,
How perfect you were...
And how we were

Did we turn people's heads?
As we walked, holding hands,
I really enjoyed it if we did...
To have you by my side

You made me seem so tall
So strong and invincible,
Just to show you off...
Was all I cared to do

To show the world
You were my love,
If that were my only job...
I thought I did it pretty well

I still smile when you cross my mind
So I guess that should say something,
But were we really perfect...
My memory surely thinks so

RANDOM RHYMES FOR DIFFERENT DAYS, DIFFERENT TIMES

Juice in Phone
About to succumb
Good night, Facebook—
"Oh, hello, rum!"

Said *goodbye* to a coworker
He seemed a nice young gent…
But his slurping coffee drove me nuts
And I'm just glad he went!

I was struck by surprise
By her pretty brown eyes
…the many-a downfall of kings…
But she's working at Hooters
With playful protruders
So, I smiled as she gave me my wings!

SWEET NOTHINGS' POEMS

Lips will hold food in your mouth
As you chew and crunch and gnaw
Lips can hide a crooked smile
Or sip soda from a straw...

But I never thought what fun they'd be—
Or of that resounding tasty "smack!"
Until my lips kissed upon your lips
And yours did kiss me back!

You've moved inside my heart
You've turned my lows to highs
My eyes are tearing up
'Cause I've got you here in my eyes

SOME OF THE WOMEN WERE KIND...

(Inspired by Mojitos and Prepared for a Song)

I forged ahead on the road less traveled
I didn't know what I wouldn't find...
I tripped on some rocks
Damn those stumbling blocks
But some of the women were kind...
Yes, some of the women were kind

When the mornings came early
Due to nights that were long
The sunshine would kiss me goodnight...
The sun would emit an orangey hue
And I'm so happy you're here, aren't you?

The days that I counted when you said goodbye
I wondered how I didn't cry...
I slept and I drank
With no one to thank
For deep inside I can't lie...
Yes, deep inside I couldn't lie

I found an old picture before we did meet
Of long-ago days—and I smiled...
But the smile was lost youth
But to tell you the truth
I remember some women were kind...
Yes, some of those women were kind

I think of you still when I'm all alone
And I concentrate just for a while...
'Cause you were included
That never intruded
You were one who treated me kind...
Yeah, yeah—you were the one that treated me kind

UNDULATING RAIN

Ah, rain
That undulating sound
Whether heavy or soft
On grass or pavement
The sound rejuvenates
Nourishing Mother Earth
Soothing rhythm
Permeating the soul
Tapering off to little droplets
Creeks and rivers drink and swell
The never-ending journey of each drop
Flowing effortlessly to the ocean

SOFT SUMMER RAIN

Rain. Soft summer rain. Tapping the outer window and sliding off the window sill nourishing the grass below. Summer rain. Gently caressing downhill, the vacant beveled streets. Flowing freely after the long journey from the heavens. A glorious ride. Making its way down the creeks in the valleys, effortlessly joining the streams and rivers. Making its way home… to Mother Ocean.

THE SECRET TO HAPPINESS

The secret to happiness is, I think
Not just joy that's from within…
But if you become disoriented
Here is where to begin:

First recognize just what you feel
And if it isn't right…
Turn up the corners of your lips—
And express just sheer delight!

Now close your eyes and hold that thought
And feel what all need's freeing…
Breathe in the joy within and out—
Allow to permeate your being

Now share that feeling with a nod
And a simple little smile…
That feeling you thought you must've lost
Was with you all the while

IF I WASN'T AFRAID

I am afraid, but I know that I shouldn't
For if I was not I could do what I wouldn't

My shackles and chains are simply imaginary…
They're merely my thoughts that bind me contrary

If I could see them, and find they are real
I could touch them, control them and be free of this wheel

But thoughts are a prison
Where I can't overcome…
I know they are false,
Make me forget where I'm from…

I'm from all the heavens, around and above…
Where all that exists, exists due to love

"*Be thankful* within…appreciate each drop of the sea
And no time at all—you'll find yourself *free!*"

THE END...THE BEGINNING

The end. The story is over. The cast of character's fade.
But your memory is clear and enlightened.
Like death, the story is over, but the library is vast. The story is infinite.
You smile.

EXHAUSTED...

Sleep, it calls me...
The warmth of slumber
Adrift inside a harbor safe
Slowly fading, into the
Abyss...

Rising, and surrounded by gentle wings
Cradled into a blissful dream
Sleep. Tranquil, peaceful, sleep

FORGOTTEN DREAM

I'd forgotten how much I loved you
My worries filled up my dreams
My painted visions were permeated by outside
Annoyances
The pigment of my brush dulled
You've been too far from my thoughts
Until a violent night that shook my being
And I awoke in a sweat…
You were no longer here with me
I have lost you, I am overwrought
The visions which brought you forth
Have now placed us asunder
I am despondent with grief
I will now turn away
I will now turn away from the vision of divisiveness
I will now turn away from the vision of petulance
And I will reacquaint myself to the Dream I lost
The Dream of your likeness
The Dream of your touch
The Dream of the hopefulness you instilled in me
That Dream
That Dream that brought you forth
And your song will again—
Banish my loneliness
And I will again have you in my Dream
And my Dream will be realized
I will no longer forget

LOST

I'm lost in love
It's all around and yet I'm lost
I followed...I watched and still remained...
No closer than arm's length
I committed once and lost my way...
As the road...it turned away
Though I thought my love was true
I found myself alone
I travel on without a path
No variance, no familiarity
Just steady and true the lonely course
Remaining ever fearless
Full of hope remaining steadfast
Never compromising. Traveling swiftly
But traveling. Ever traveling.

REALITY IN ANOTHER PARADIGM

The following was inspired while listening to Swami Vidyadhishananda Giri at West Virginia State, Ferrell Hall, on June 26, 2008. He said that what "we" find as paranormal is considered normal in the Himalayas. The title was actually *his words* as he spoke of life in the Himalayas.

Someone asked, "*How do you properly meditate*" and he said, with a heavy accent, "Just sit and smile." I expect he meant not just from within, but also from without (outside)

Restrained in human body form and anchored here on earth
Life ends as we know it…as we enlighten toward rebirth

Past lives become as one, from within and now without
That on earth, was not to be—now will leave no doubt

Human knowledge clouded, cloaked awareness overturned
Rediscovered, reawakened…received and now discerned

Earthly darkness put asunder, now ambient insight grows
Awareness that was hidden, stagnate knowledge flows

The loneliness of mother earth takes another form
That which couldn't…but now is
Paranormal's now the norm

BLUE ARE THE EYES

Blue are the eyes as I gaze into heaven,
Some say a ten or even eleven!

Green are the eyes that seem to be mean…
But are they really? Remains to be seen

But *brown* are the eyes, so soft and so warm,
Bring into me vigor. I feel I'm reborn!

All of the colors, which are most kind,
It isn't the color, it's what lies behind!

TERRA FIRMA PRELUDE

Sent from the other side, born a terrestrial being…
For lessons to be learned—more knowing, more seeing

A mere human child, a screaming infant
Like so many others, no more, no different

(In which way to go) "Which road is my choice"
(Was I told once before, where I once heard a voice)

From heaven to earth, my direction seems lost…
For direction I'll pay, "But will I afford this cost"

I share now just loneliness how long must I conceal that
I'm weary and I'm angry, "Was this part of the deal"

My path needs cleared, but somewhere…inside…
The answer lies deep, where it successfully hides

So, on my way, my gift—my gift I've last viewed….
Time, now to be spent, in this earthly prelude

I'll feel abandoned just left in the dust…
But I'll place faith in G-d…and turn my fear into trust

CRYPTIC LIGHT

Down a lonely corridor shone
A shimmering ray of light
It gave forth to me a cryptic tone—
A still and silent sight

I gazed upon with queried wonder
And cautious puzzled thought...
I couldn't tell just what it was
Or what it may have brought

I moved ahead, on toward the light
It seemed to lead me on...
A feeling seemed secure at first
Than dance around withdrawn

This cryptic light is "life," I thought
A compass...if I'm lost...
A ship in port—and then at sea
And to the winds I'm tossed

I cannot know the answer here
Until more time I spend...
To sail in waters still unknown
Unto my journey's end

The beacon sent to lead me on
This straight or varied course...
The queried light still leads me forth
But remains in shadows force

I need to plot a steady course
To cut through this mystique
Until the light reveals to me
The answers that I seek

OUT OF BODY EXPERIENCE

My dreams have evaporated
A lifeless outer shell...
I close my eyes to find my way
Outside this lonely hell!

The day it drifts away
Sleep permeates my being...
Deeper down I spiral down
In darkness without seeing

But a wispy little nudge
And then a stronger poke...
I felt my breath get snatched away
As I began to choke

I felt a rush of euphoria
With the absence of bright light...
Still, the feeling was intense
As I saw within the night

My eyes could see myself
Lay below in strife...
Is this the end of life on Earth?
Towards joyous afterlife

I saw myself in struggle
Wrestling with my role...
Though while I witness my duress
I rose above in soul

Not a single worry
No deadlines had to meet...
Just *a simple all around*
feeling that was sweet

Yet what I saw below
That earthly human toil...
Struggling, to breathe again
From perpetual turmoil

I'm not quite sure I'm ready
For terrestrial passage out...
Even though just what I felt
I couldn't do without

Yet through my weary struggle
I thought I'm not quite done...
My soul it must return itself
And reunite as one

I know that something's out there...
I've seen and felt and dreamed it
My choice to disembark this ride
Will soon enough permit

I'm anticipating when
Euphoria reappears...
If days or weeks or months are left
Or I wait for many years

No matter what's ahead
My focus should be here...
Along with lonely earthly bound
And find those I hold dear

So, cleanse my inner being
And show me inner light…
Help me to regain my soul
And restore impassioned sight

Thank you for this little gift
the gift of "all is well…"
It taught me I've no place to fear
And led me out of hell.

AFTERLIFE

Once the veil of love is lifted
In that time—knowledge is gifted

Enduring burdens so much tougher
From earthly burdens that we all suffer

Hatred and difference here are shared
Lifts the veil with all repaired

Here we lie with weighted fodder
Until the light will flow like water

Enveloping knowledge scatters above
The only knowledge—is that of love

SEAWEED IN THE SURF

Seaweed in the surf
That was the plan
To go with the flow
As best as I can

But the road it veered
Away from course
Where others *dared* not
Away from their source

The plans they were changed
And my dreams unraveled
I'm onto the path
Of the road less traveled

Smooth and straight
From the formative years
Not quite expecting
The river of tears

No longer expected
Each curve a surprise
The road less traveled
Became my demise

Until in the distance
A foreign thought found
From deep in a crevice
A whispering sound

Repeatedly faint
Until I can find
A small recognition
From deep in my mind

Just forge ahead
And make my own path
The road less traveled
Had lost all its wrath

I imagined the way
And there it was wrought
A tiny old lesson
Of once I was taught

The seaweed that flowed
Aimlessly about
Became the purpose
That I was without

Wherever I go
And no matter what
To live as I am
Without a shortcut

RELIGIOUS RHETORIC

Some of you have read my posts
And some are horrified…
To some my words may resonate,
While some wish, I'd abide.

Religious rhetoric is not my thing
Though my spirituality exists…
I loathe when peaceful sacred words,
Are used with hateful twists.

See the ones with pointed finger
Claiming—only *they* are just…
If that's the case I turn my back,
On whomever they lay trust…

What I know and what I feel
From your hurtful laden preach…
Are not what I would pass along,
To others I would teach.

Live your life; keep to yourself
Your venom laden hiss…
Leaving those to live their own—
And mind your own business!

MISTRUST

Once you feel you place your trust
With those that you've thought friends
Only soon to learn about
Their friendship just depends

Soon again to realize
The faith in those you gave
Only that you're just a pawn
To serve as if a slave

Betrayal felt within myself
Another sordid thought
The anger of my stupid trust
I never should have brought

NO MONEY

What would you do
If there was no money
Would you continue to worry?
Wouldn't that be funny

What would you do
Without your things,
Would you turn your attention?
And see what that brings

What would you do
If your interest would turn
Would you begin to grow?
What more could you learn

What would you do
By loosening strings
Empowering others
And giving them wings

If there was no money
What would you do
If currency grew
With each good deed that you do

What would you do
If there was no money
Would the earth's disposition
Start to turn out sunny

All our lives
It hasn't been funny
But wouldn't it be great
If we didn't need money

CLOSED DOOR

The door that never opened…
Remained quite tightly closed
Revealing only status quo—
Opportunity unexposed

Searching for another door—
Elusive so it seems…
The only one I find ajar—
Is found within my dreams

That door never opened
Remains quite tightly shut
But I still breathe, in and out
And knock no matter what

WHAT WOULD I REGRET

If I died tomorrow
What would I regret
Is there someone in my past?
Or someone I've not met

That I could say a simple word
To lift their spirit up?
Or maybe do a little task
And fill their empty cup

If I died tomorrow
Would it have been worthwhile?
Only if each day I try
To make somebody smile

THE VOICES

I hear these voices in my head
I wished they'd go away
They tell me that I'm just "no good"
They've nothing good to say

There're times when I believe in them
They draw me deeper in despair
Seeming so insistent—
Strangled in a spider's lair

I try to think of other things
To get them off my mind
But I just can't seem to see my way
I'm trapped as if I'm blind

But I know what the remedy is
I've known it all along
I reach way down within myself
And I find my sacred song

My song is nothing ordinary
To me it saves my life
It strikes down all the make-believe
Those voices and their strife

When I adhere to my own song
The one that speaks the truth
No voice will then intimidate
No matter how uncouth

My song within is just a smile
Breathing in and breathing out
It gives me all the strength I need
And arms me from without

I place my song inside my head
With intention to allow
To put my smile upon my face
And live life in the now

If you gaze into a mirror
And it only takes a while
Those voices that are in our head
Extinguish as you smile

DREAMS IN MY SLUMBER

In my slumber
I had this dream
Vague at first
A typical scene

The other side
Revealed itself
This classic book
From a dusty shelf

This typical dream
A nonsensical wonder
But no pirate treasure
No pillage, no plunder

The haze soon cleared
To become quite vivid
But my senses feel prodded
And I begin to feel "livid"

All of a sudden
My whole being shook
My eyes aren't open
And yet I could look

A message is brought
Though I still can't believe
I must still be in slumber
This dream to deceive

Just like the rest
I hoped for an answer
But answers are cloaked
Like inside of a cancer

Not a disease
Just mere happenstance
No question, no answer
Just sheer annoyance

A force once was clear
As clear as a bell
But now clutter engulfs
This crusty eggshell

Now wait! I had thought
An egg brings forth life!
Included within
There's the joy and the strife

It still makes no sense
This egg and this dream
I'm inside—I'm now outside
Without compass or stream

I'm lost yet again
With my fists plainly guarded
I'm tired—I'm weary
And feel disregarded

Again…once revealed
The answers in slumber…
But, again I'm deceived
Yet still I encumber

IN THE NOW

As we glance around not taking time
To hear and see without
We miss the things important for us
To laugh and sing about

But if we listen, really, really listen
To what the soul says from within
And live our life set in the now
Instead of where it's been

DYING AND REBIRTH

(Journey Toward the Afterlife)

Omnipotent euphoria
As I'm drawn so high
Gazing down and all around
I feel the other side

I see below my withered self
Tethered by the Earth
Terrestrial being left behind
And journey toward rebirth

LITTLE BLACK DRESS

Little black dress that caught my eye
With all that long dark hair
I wonder where you went
And would you take me there?

I watched you walk across the street
But I didn't get a chance
To see you to your destination
Or catch a frontal glance

I noticed you were passing by
I watched your black dress sway
I later saw you from afar
Only blocks away

Out of park I turned my car
And into traffic I sped
I watched you turn around the bend
But I could not dart ahead

So, I lost that little black dress
With the hair, so dark and wild
But thank you as you made my day
And all day long I smiled!

YOU'RE IN MY DREAMS AGAIN

Once again you entered my dreams
More real than the time before
I could smell your scent on my pillow
My senses began to soar

You were wispy and you were luminous
Your form glowed from deep inside
I felt your soul quite infinite
I held out my arms as wide

I wrapped my arms around you
I breathed in your essence deep
You melted into my being
My joy caused me to weep

I stroked your face with my finger
I felt the softness of your skin
I lifted your chin to mine
And kissed you again and again

I tasted your salty lips
And the sweetness of your tongue
I caressed your entire body
I felt us become one

I believed my joy was realized
Until the piercing of my eyes
The sun knifed through my window
And vanquished you, my prize

Lying here in afterthought
Still lost from where I'd been
But slowly smile and anticipate
When I hold you once again!

THE SWEETEST FACE

The sweetest little face
I let pass by my fate
I tried to engage a thought
But she chose not to wait

That sweetest little face
Still weighs upon my mind
But vision's always 20/20
When looking from behind

The sweetest little face
I still give wistful thought
If I should have welcomed you
Just what you would have brought?

My sweetest little face
I bid you sweet adieu
I'll think of you in slumber
And in my dreams pursue

SOMETHING ABOUT YOU

I only needed a woman
It didn't have to be you
You caught and held my attention
There was just something about you

I looked away more than a few times
But my gaze came back to you
The more I tried to divert myself
My thoughts steered back to you
…And I like it

I SAW HER

I saw her in a college hall
Not so long ago
Looking like a work of art
Painted by Van Gogh

Attending informal deliberation
She flashed a joyful smile
Then ended up in back of time
Right behind my aisle

I took a glance whenever I could
I quickly showed my bias
Between debate or watching her
I think I made it obvious

Then I heard a little roar
The crowd bestowed a laugh
But through it all I heard the sound
Or just her own behalf

She laughed with so much fervor
Her entire body shook
I had to take another glance
And have another look

I quickly made my way toward her
After the debate
Darting out and through the crowd
Before it was too late

The talk was small and through it all
I found myself beguiled
For as she turned and walked away
Her head turned back and smiled

I'll never really know for sure
If she was smiling at me
Or if I may have thought astray
And she was really laughing at me

DRUGSTORE LADY POEM

Lady stranger in the drugstore aisle
I've thought of you for quite a while

You turned and smiled as I strode by
I quickly left and wondered why

Why I didn't stop and just ask
Why I didn't—that simple task

It's been days and you're still a thought
Of what a simple phrase may have brought

But now you're gone, as am I
What could've been, if I just said, "Hi!"

The following was written within the last few months *before* I knew Sheila E...was coming to Charleston. They were written for a cousin of hers...Jenny, from Stockton, California. I knew her when I was stationed at the Naval Communication Station.

FOR YOU, MY DEAR...

I hope you remember
Cause I won't forget
Those days that we laughed
And the night that we met

Our time was too short
The distance so long
I still smile for you
When I hear your song

At nights, I look up
And pick out a star
I'm thinking of you
Wondering where you are

I still feel inside
But won't let it show
It's not meant for all
It's just for you to know

Next time I'm outside
Again, seeking that star
My heart will still ache
And harbor your scar

The future will hold
That you are my prize
And my reflection I see
In your lustrous dark eyes

No need to forgive
We've already done that
I'll think of you often
And the love we begat

So, for you, my dear
When the stars all align
I'll again be yours
And again, you'll be mine

WORDS

I want to write a poem
For all the world to see
In hopes that someone
Passes on-
For my beloved to see;

Words relay a simple verse
Intention without revealing
Of whom or what the motive is
Or if it's most appealing

A cryptic code relays itself
The still unknown intended
As if my words will find someone
Or maybe just pretended

Regardless of the cloak and dagger
My heart will still traverse
All balled-up in peaceful wish
Into the universe

I've written you poems
I've written you sonnets
Beyond the stars
Asteroids, and comets

A time now lost
Before today
A long-ago year
A different day

Then I awoke
I exhale and realize
You were just a dream
And I close my eyes

My dearest muse
I can only pretend
That you're back in my arms
And my heart starts to mend

I'll gather my letters
My verse and rhyme
I'll gather the poems
My resonant chime

Those words that I wrote
That enlightened my view
Please stay by my side
And I'll read them to you

When I C u again

ONLINE DATING

Disguised inside these varied words
A life condensed profile
Are hidden thoughts for you to find?
And bring about a smile

The relationship key is truly tough
To mold and stretch to fit
Until you find the right keyhole
And then your flame is lit

To find the right relationship
Can sometimes be futile
But when you know—you will know
To stroll on down the aisle

Encouraged to date online
Because I was such a catch
But eHarmony and OkCupid
Seemed kind a stupid
So maybe I could try Match

But I thought and pondered
And like my people I wandered
But not in a barren desert
I'm not wanting a shiksa
So, I mixed an elixa
And to JDate, I would revert

So, I drafted a profile
And this little rhyme
To see just what would become
Of a dating creation
And possible relation
Or maybe, just have some fun!

DATING

Dating with no dough
Where would we go
If I asked you out?

Without any bread
Would you leave me instead?
And I'll be left here to pout

THE MORNING AFTER A JIMMY BUFFETT CONCERT

The sun came through my window this morning
Saying, "It's time to arise!"
I enlightened my friend: "A long night was had"
And continued on to apprise

I explained why I was up so late
Hoping that he'd understand
"What precluded any slumber was
A musical number—
Jimmy Buffett and his Coral Reefer Band!"

The sun just smiled and continued to shine
And then the blinds he drew…
For he and the wind, the sea and the stars
Well, apparently, "They're Parrot Heads, too!"

IS THIS THE BEGINNING OF SOMETHING!

Let me take you on a trip
A trip to the horizon
Flying toward a lighted moon
Until the sun is risin'

A simple little trip I plan
For just the two of us
Where time alone is what we'll share
And deepest dreams discuss

LOVE IS EXPENSIVE

Worth it

The loves we lost
Or perhaps misplaced
Between a romance
What once was untraced

The wonder "what if?"
Is the annoying constant
If what was once sunk
Can now become buoyant

4. NAUTICAL

SAILOR ROB PROLOGUE

(Children's Book Idea)

Aboard the S. S. *Juanita*
A course plotted to explore
The harbor sounds surround him
As he prepares to leave the shore

He hoists his anchor for Scotland
Visiting the Lowlands and the Highlands
Sail through the Isthmus of Panama
And off to the Philippine Islands

He loves the art of sailing
And just to see how fast
He circumnavigates his ship
About the world so vast

From the continent of Africa
With his first mate nicknamed "Chief"
Around the Cape of Good Hope—
Ahead to the Great Barrier Reef

So, gather up your dreams
And securely stow your gear
And muster all aboard
As we sail both far and near

Armed with sextant and sail
It's time for "Anchors Aweigh,"
Shore leave now expired
It's five knots out the bay

He likes to learn all that he can
From every Port of Call
And then it's back home for leave
Telling stories, one and all

"NEVER GO DRINKING UNTIL THE SUN IS PAST THE HIGHEST YARDARM, DEPENDING ON WHERE YOU STAND, IT'S ALWAYS PAST THE HIGHEST YARDARM"

Never go drinking
(But with one eye that's winking)
Till the sun's past the highest yardarm…

'Cause depending where you stand
Whether at sea or on land—
You're always past that yardarm!

Before "Five O'Clock Somewhere"
They were already aware—
Imbibing before hearing that song!

Raising their glass
As the rum they did pass—
The Sailors knew all along…

"It's 5 O'Clock" or so the song goes
And what that means – we know
But years before
I knew the score
With this secret I shall disclose…

My sailing days I honed my skills
With tradition and nautical charm
Rum was our beverage
And also, our leverage
When the sun passed the highest yardarm

We'd stop and we'd look
Above to our ships' tallest mast
Regulation did prescribe
We would never imbibe
'Til that sun would slowly move past

But with the cunning of the sailor
We were always ready and manned
For this salty old crowd
Knew what we were allowed
And then we'd move from where we did stand

SUNSET ON SIESTA KEY, FLORIDA

Lonesome sunset on the sea
The sailor plots his course
The vessel's diminished sight askew
And vanished from its source

Blanketed into gentle night
Kissed the sun adieu
Nestled into clouded sky
Beyond horizon's view

Familiar shores are left behind
With friends and loved ones too
The lonesome Sailor's farewell bid
Of things that he once knew

On his own, he rekindles forth
Ocean's familiar caress
Her temperamental soothing tides
Or waves that cause duress

Mother Ocean and the Sailor
Kinship of ancient days
Along with the stars and moon above
Not soon to part their ways

HAPPY BIRTHDAY, USMC

(From the Navy to the Jarheads on November 10th each Year)

They've oft been called 'those Devil Dogs'
As they dress in their camouflage greens...
But if you see one today—
Bestow a *happy birthday!*
For the few, the proud, the Marines!"

Semper fi!

SAIL

Ocean blue, ocean blue
Sailing course—
Steady and true

Ocean gray, ocean gray
Stormy squalls, on their way

Ocean teal and sunny feel...
Shallow waters, warm and surreal

Reflecting water off the sky
Reaching prism of the eye

SEAFARER'S JOURNEY

Sunburned skin in frayed canvas raft
Floating adrift a slight six-inch draft

Mother ship sailed without keeping time
As I drift away, from safe paradigm

Peaceful and calm—the crest of a wave
Down in a valley—or watery grave

It started in days then grew into years
Along with some smiles accompanied by tears

Chasing and following the horizon's soft lure
In quest of an answer to abandonment's cure

Time is a fleeting like flowing cascades
Years combined now—in lonesome decades

Unknown to me, I'm now in the trades
A course is now set—and onward pervades

Defeated horizon—revealing ahead
Some unknown land, no longer misleads

A newfound vigor, a resonant accord
Into safe harbor lies my reward

Formerly lost, tossed and about
With welcoming arms, I'm no longer in doubt

Gone is the fear, gone is the rancor
My sail is now stowed, and here I set anchor

THANK YOU, VETERANS!

Army, Navy, Air Force, Marines,
Coast Guard, too, by all means…

Thank you for service—you honored your country,
So, we honor you to the highest degree

Reflect on today, for your time well spent,
Thanking all those—who know what it meant

To sacrifice time and lives from loved ones,
Your husbands, your wives, your daughters, your sons

This country celebrates your devotion today,
Those serving and served for the ole' USA

On Veteran's Day, there is no dispute,
We all look to you, and offer salute

So, here's to you, from everyone,
A hearty congrats—for a job well done

WATCHFUL SAILOR

Watchful Sailor's lonesome gaze
Upon horizon's cloudy haze
Watching the ocean's undulating dance
Searching the deep and watery expanse

With thoughts of dreaming
When Independent Steaming
As water to starboard and so to port
Business as usual on a Destroyer Escort

For leagues below, thoughts coalesce
With mysterious depth, of muted darkness
Questions arise. "Just what's below?"
Eternal wonders we'll never know

THE BALLAD OF APPLE AND CHERRY

(A Sailor's Story of a Night on Liberty)

Me and Big Al went out on the town,
Partying at our best...
It was the early '80s
And Al met two ladies
Who would put us both to the test

When "the Legend," Big Al, met these two ladies,
He wasn't aware of their plan...
But "Come over" he called—
And over I hauled...
(When really...I shoulda ran!)

Introductions were exchanged,
And then, I became wary—
When these two dames
Told me their names,
"I'm Apple...and...I'm Cherry"

(I thought, "They devised their little plan,
before they left their nest...")
Then right on cue
Al asked, "Can we come, too?"
And we escorted them both to breakfast

Late at night, there at Denny's,
This, I could have missed...
When, with her finger she pointed
My wallet came disjointed
When she asked, "Can I have this?"

"Steak and eggs? Sakes alive!"
(But thought, "I could just strike it rich!")
So "Of course," I said
With the thought in my head,
It might "turn on" her toggle switch

After chow, we two sailors,
Were still very much in the chase...
But no slap and no tickle,
Getting in their vehicle—
And they headed...on toward the base!

"Which pier are you?" Cherry then asked
But we didn't even murmur...
But then instead,
We both shook our heads—
When a marine cried, "Halt, no further!"

Window down, she said, "*Hello*,"
To the Jarhead there at the gate...
Then he alluded
And there we concluded
That here, he sealed our fate

Exiting doors, now open wide,
We needed no further instruction
As they smiled from their car—
And waved. "Au revoir!"
Rejection. Our final obstruction

Being quite miffed, I harassed Big Al—
"There'd be no glimpse of heaven…"
But onward we strolled
Through a night that was cold
As we dragged-ass back to pier seven

(*Final Chapter*)
The sun it arose and all was recounted,
The story of how those two dames…
Went out on the town
And shot sailors down
Big Al, "the Legend," had gone down in flames!

A TRANQUIL NIGHT AT SEA

I never spent such a calming night
As a peaceful night at sea
The stars would sparkle all around
While looking back at me

The salty air, it fills my lungs
The breeze blows back my hair
The waves caress the hull of my ship
On plotted course somewhere

This darkened night out at sea
With mystery deep below
As stars signal with their wink
Their magical spectral show

The silent wind on peaceful sail
Envelopes all within
The sea cradles gently
Where only time has been

Thoughtful waves carry on
This beginning with no end
A lonely thought, dissipates
Knowing where and when

All is clear and all in focus
The night will see to that
By sending guiding star to lead
Atop watered habitat

Spirit's tranquil voices
Tell their sacred philosophy
Their wisdom and the courage
Of a sailor out at sea

As I witness a show of shooting stars
With the absence of light pollution
This calming peaceful sea at night
Offering remedy and absolution

5. MINDLESS MEANDERINGS

THE TELEVANGELIST

Shattering dreams to little bits
Filled by shallow Hypocrites
Religious leaders lead their sect
Gathering riches is what they collect

Listen to me and my joyous song
Shame your friends that don't come along
Cast off those friends who do not abide
Send me more money or faith be denied

SNOWSTORM EVENING

Peaceful and serene
After a winter's heavy snow...
A four-wheel drive
Proves it can thrive
Putting on a show

Sounds they carry through the night
They travel even further—
No impedance
Or interference
Soar freely, without bother...

Driven snow casting light,
Reflecting streetlight's glow...
Still the night
No soul in sight
A tranquil overthrow...

Evening drapes the blizzard's end
And quells the stormy rite...
Formerly vibrant—
Now strangely silent
Into peaceful winter's night

CONVERSING WITH THE DEAD

When talking to the dead
Convey what's in your heart
Know that they are there
And that is where you start

Speak lovingly with a smile
For it's how they're seeing you
Just close your eyes and feel them near
For they are feeling you

They give you all their love
And know that everything's all right
Believe in what they're saying
While bathing in their light

Feel yourself be healed
All your worries drift away
Smile and breathe both in and out
Each and every day

Feel deep in your soul
The love that they bestow
And don't forget to return the favor
It's what will help you grow

So, as you go through life
Upon this earthly plane
Know that they are always there
In sunshine and in rain

THANKS FOR ABUNDANCE

It is in giving that we receive
As we sow abundantly,
We reap abundantly
This is the divine law

As I give and share generously and abundantly
My life is blessed with great financial,
And material prosperity

Money flows to me easily, constantly
And in great abundance,
Whatever I invest comes back to me
Many, many times

My life is blessed with
So much abundance,
So much prosperity
So much success

I am blessed with tremendous prosperity
And I lived a life of moderation,
Discipline and spirituality

I am healthy and very happy
I am enjoying every moment of my life

May every person, every being be blessed with
Good health, happiness, prosperity, and spirituality

With thanks and in full faith. So be it.

MIDNIGHT BUS RIDE

Moonlight through the bus window shines
As the engine hums, sputters, and whines

Onward journey through the night
Destination miles from sight

As Jupiter appears to court the moon
I consider the stars and their lover's swoon

Shadows grow both short and long
As rubber and road spin their song

Flickered lights from passing towns
Wave their greeting with silent sounds

Silhouettes of hills and trees
As bus ride continues—won't you please?

Make this journey offer deep counsel
And compose an end that's peaceful

FOUR LINES IN MY NAVY TERVIS TUMBLER

(Special thanks for the inspiration from Howard Livingston and Mile Marker 24, although, I really suspect he wouldn't want the credit. Hear his song: "Four Lines in a Tervis Tumbler" off his album, Six Pack and a Tan!)

Morning sun shines through my window
Arise for a weekend in summer…
Morning chores and thoughts to later
Of two lines in my *Tall Tervis Tumbler*

The winter's cold has been placed on hold
To sleep during warm weather slumber…
Still my thoughts—of a refreshing drink
Two lines in my *Tall Tervis Tumbler*

Running errands to store number one
I'm in for a heartbreaking bummer…
Spying a sight of sweet little honey
She certainly was a cute little number

She turned and strode into another aisle
Where I guess, I started to feel humbler…
And alas again, she turned away-
Now three lines in my *Tall Tervis Tumbler*

So, on my way to store number two
To mix rum into my tumbler…
But first through the rain as I made my way—
Are thoughts where I felt like a bumbler

Yet as I was mixin', the thought of that vixen
Made my heart beat like that of a drummer....
So, I smiled and toasted to that long-legged
Honey—
With four lines of rum in my *Tall Tervis Tumbler.*

DOG SITTING

Dog sittin' for a friendly neighbor
With rum poured in my chalice
I feel like that Jimmy Buffett song
With those "Gypsies in the Palace!"

There hasn't been a party
But if I had one wish
The cleanup wouldn't be too bad
Though I already broke one dish

Their dog and I would walk
Down the street and near a loop
I'd whip out a baggy and made it quite saggy
As I picked up Fido's poop!

But evenings were sedate
No raucous—not even a peep
Nothing was heard at all from that pooch—
Until I tried to sleep

A fifteen-year old dog
That's 105 for us
Like an old man sitting down
He'd groan and moan and fuss

Each time he'd change positions
I'd hear a muffled yelp
As if to say that "I'm right here"
But that he didn't need my help

He followed from room to room
And we got along so well
That next time there will be a party
Since I'm sure he wouldn't tell!

MONDAY MORN...

It's Monday morn'
So, don't be late
C'mon, clock!
'Cause I can't wait!"

Just breathe in for now
And then breathe out...
Friday's there
Please leave no doubt

An act of congress
Could move those days
Move Fridays closer
And we'd give them praise!

But then they'd raise their pay
As if we never knew
Then they'd give us a break
And take us outta that, too!

DAYDREAMING AT NIGHT IN TEXAS

Reflected water on lake house glass
Sunlight's descent, not to be its last

Tomorrow begins a fresh new morn'
The sun will rise again, reborn

Still, rays on the water glisten
And present an eve of new whisper to listen...

The night will gently fall as it always does,
To revive anything you desire, anything that was...

LAKE HOUSE DREAMIN'

No pirate sails, no guns a thunder
Just beverage and breeze to quell any plunder

The rays of sunshine skip on the lake
Good company and laughter will cure any ache

A song on the wind, a gentle ambient caress
Another solution for any duress

A faint lap of water upon the lakeshore
It'll soon be done, and I'll yearn for some more

TEXAS

Don't mess with Texas
That's all we did hear
Then strolled into town
Team Mountaineer!

With Woods and with Buie
And Bailey and Tavon
These young Mountaineers
Arrived with their game on

But leading them all
The man and the myth
The Heisman hopeful
Our own Geno Smith

Longhorns bewildered
With runs and with passes
Geno Smith's legend
Befuddled their masses

Largest crowd ever
Witnessed this night
No help from above
When they screamed, "Texas fight!"

Geno prevailed
When all's said and done
The Mountaineer faithful
Had finally won!

Now off to Sixth Street
Celebrating en masse
And a cheer for the "Horns
That showed us such class"

I hope that next year
When they come to our town
We serve them our best
And they won't leave with a frown

We won't hide our manners
In a kangaroo's pouch
But bestow them our gratitude
As we light up a couch

But I say this aloud
What I just said in jest
Show these fine folks
Mountaineers fans are best!

THE PREQUEL TO TEXAS POEM

We answered the phone when the Big 12 called
And went out to the Midwest to play
We packed up our bags and stowed our gear
And flew into Texas that day

SUVs full with the Mountaineer faithful
As we cruised out from DFW
And at our very first stop was not just typical slop
But genuine Texas BBQ!

After ribs and taters and steaks and chops
We shopped east of the 100th meridian
And lo and behold at the local box store
We ran into a fellow Charlestonian!

Next the long drive to a big Texas lake
We're lucky that Harry didn't wreck
When Smallridge pulled out his little black book
And introduced us to Stacy Wrecht

We finally arrived and picked our rooms
Tired from traveling all day
But that didn't stop us from turning around
For dinner—the *Texican* way

With guacamole and frijoles at Ochoa's, I think
They fed the whole Mountaineer tribe
More chips and salsa and margaritas and tequila
The crew began to imbibe

But then after a good night's rest
We got up to a great big beautiful morn
Time on the lake, then we broke out the steaks
And grilled us a Texas Longhorn!

We all had such a grand ole' time
With our cracks, jokes, and quips
Nobody knew before that day
That Marc had really soft lips!

We filled out our roster the very next day
With the man already on the scene
The one and the only
Parkersburg's Tavon" Goldstein

That night we carried on and on
As if we were up on Sunnyside
Then off to bed for the long day ahead
In store for another long ride

Reveille at five with the Pride of West Virginia
By Gary————which I thought was cruel
But after a few minutes I gained my composure
And thought, "Man, that's pretty cool!"

We packed up our stuff and began the trek
To Austin we set out to deploy
But with too much to drink and without any sink
We got "Chud" all over our convoy!

Fortunately, though, we had Doctor Greg
To assess and prescribe him a cure
So, he sent Chud to bed with a pill for his head
And so, his vision would no longer blur

Now what lay ahead with the facts and the figures
Already laid down in the annals of history…
Even that big Texas drum could not overcome
What ended in Mountaineer victory!

DOCTOR'S OFFICE

Waiting in the "waiting room"
Waiting in the patient's room
Wondering if the doc will ever come

It wouldn't be so awful
If only staff would offer
A little bitty shot or two of rum!

VOTE THEM OUT!

I don't know why
But it's time for a verse
After watching the news
I just wanna curse

Congress is snug
Like big ole' fat cats
Taking more than their share
From us little lab rats

They make up the laws
Which serve only themselves
And expect us to be grateful
Like Santa's little elves

Until we respond
By gathering clout
To stop all their madness
And vote their ass out!

ELECTION POEM

The election is finally over
I look for a reprieve
But now the talks, the squawks, the balks—
Will claim, "We've been deceived!"

So here we go—for all to know
It's about to get repeated
For now, the loser, those—his choosers—
Will cry, "Hey—those guys, they cheated!"

So, another topic—far from tropic
Will not emerge on this
For we're controlled and pigeonholed
To repeat again this mess!

TEXAS FLIGHTS

Not wanting to visit my past
I'm southbound to have me a blast
This may sound screwy
But I'm near "my ex" in St. Louie
And I wanna get outta here fast!

DOG DAY IN TEXAS

A different perspective as the sun clips the trees
Ceiling fans stir by a warm Texas breeze

A screen door sounds as the dog slips through
Today's his day off without much to do

Ready to pounce at any beck and call
For a sudden alarm or fiercely thrown ball

He answers all who come to scoff—
What does a dog do on his day off!

(Inspired by George Carlin and Texas Sunset)

KEY WEST ADVENTURE

With billowy gray skies and the air quite tropical
Armed with coconut and pineapple, in rum and some topical

Sunny and balmy on south Florida beaches
For miles and miles, and as far as he reaches

All encompassed along this stretch
Of swampy land for a high price fetch

Deep in the gulf and surviving the Atlantic
It stretches on south encompassing all that's romantic

Sweet mojitos and Cuban empanadas
Tinged Latin rhymes in steamy armadas

Guided by lighthouse the ancient mariner
Arrives ashore no longer a foreigner

Excitement builds into a crescendo
My intended destination without innuendo

Cayo Hueso translated—Bone Island
The highest elevation, a sixteen-foot highland

The palm trees stand strong
Enticing for all to join along

The watery beauty seen through sunglasses
Deepest greens with turquoise patches

A revelry ensued without much debauchery
A haunted mystery and a pleasant cacophony

Last breath of humid air with undulating sound
The island music still wafts as I commence to rebound

Filled with ignited vigor and freed from all indenture
I secure my lines and stow my gear then plan my next adventure

6. PEOPLE
(POEMS FOR FRIENDS AND
FAMILY THROUGH THE YEARS)

RICHARD'S BIRTHDAY

Gather ye, Parrot Heads
And wish all together
A birthday among us
Despite the cold weather

The leader among us
Ensures we all flock
When Bubba's in town
We sing and we squawk

Shout from the hilltops
From Seattle to Trenton
Happy birthday to you—
Our own Richard Fenton!

MOTHERS' DAY

I do my best to share some words
To express what's deep within
And hope you feel our gracious love
But where do I begin?

Though a "thanks" is not enough—
For what you give us every day
All we have are these mere words
Of what our hearts convey

The words I want you to feel
As the sentiment remains the same
Because when smiles and love are all around
You're the one to blame!

Happy Mother's Day!

HAPPY BIRTHDAY TO MY COUSIN RUTH

To my good-lookin' cousin Ruth,
We want you to tell us the truth…
It's not that we mind it—
But Ponce de Leon couldn't find it
So, where'd *you* find the Fountain of Youth?

POEM FOR AMANDA

Best wishes for you in Cleveland—
Where the Cuyahoga was once ablaze
But please remember us in Charleston—
Where your smile would make our days

But when cold winds begin to howl
And the lake rolls in a storm…
Think of us…as we'll think of you
And our thoughts will keep you warm!

JACKIE AND MELISSA

Facebook tells me now,
About these girls from school…
Many, many, years ago-
Man! They are so cool!

I see they share a birthday,
Before, I never knew…
But due to social media—
Facebook says they do!

So happy birthday, Jackie!
And Melissa, to you, too…
You both defy ole' Father Time
And bid his job adieu!

Cheers!

I've been alerted
To what can't be averted
Of two ladies sharing today…
To Jackie and Mel
Who formed a cartel
By keeping your years at bay

Your secrets of beauty
Make it my duty
To question the years that you hid…
But I've lifted the veil
And according to scale
You two are way off the grid!

You ladies are still looking as beautiful as ever—*Cheers!*

GUIDO

Happy birthday, Guido
Hope today's good for your libido…
But for you, my friend,
I do not recommend—
That you should ever be seen wearing a Speedo!

TO MARCY

*(Hi, Marcy, I hope you received my card and enjoyed the poem,
If not how 'bout this one)*

I send you best wishes and to
Lighten your mood if it's heavy…
To hoist a few, whether wine or brew
And join us at Live on the Levee!

KATHY

They say birthdays put lines on your face
And you no longer can keep up the pace...
But that's just a myth...
When it comes to Miss Smith
'Cause it just isn't true in her case!

MATTIE'S FIFTIETH

Throughout the years, once seemed perennial,
Though now you've turned a half centennial

So, let's all go back to a time once forgotten,
To a time "I barely remember" (and hope not *verboten*)

A time much simpler, we had no electronics,
Although if we did, we were labeled moronics

Television did add some spice before slumber
'Course there were lots less channels (remember the number?)

Do you recall…Spotlight, Mother May I, and ole' Simon Says?
Old men wearing hats with that silly old "fez?"

Having to "dress" to go out-in "public" by all means,
Our parents would just die, if they saw us in jeans!

When Kentucky Fried Chicken was at the bottom of the hill,
You liked drumsticks, too—so I couldn't eat my fill

The Carpenters, your favorite, I remember them well—
And Close-Up toothpaste—so our breath didn't smell

Happy birthday, I love you…my dear cousin, you'll always be…
Yeah…I'm just teasin'—though you're *way* older than me!

MISTI

'Twasn't so very long in the past—
You lived upstairs, and we all had a blast

When pups weren't soundproof—
And then two found the roof—
But through it all—you were never outclassed!

Happy birthday!

HAPPY BIRTHDAY, MOM

Happy birthday to my Mom,
Now on the other side…
I never thanked you for your time
And all that you supplied

You tried to teach me manners,
Instill upon me chivalry…
You set the tone to live my life
To such a high degree

But even through the chaos,
You ensured that all was calm…
And though I didn't show it then
I'm proud you were my mom!

CAROLYN, THROUGH THE YEARS

Happy birthday to Carolyn Faber,
My formerly East-Ended neighbor…
A hospital employee,
But you travel so constantly—
That I'm checking with the department of labor!

Happy birthday to Carolyn Faber,
In 1961, our moms were in labor…
And those lessons we took—
From Ms. Givens to Miss Cook,
And now I call the Clampetts my neighbor!

I'm sorry I arrived late…
But banker's hours aren't so great,
But a birthday for Carolyn—
I had to come barrelin'
And wish many more to be *great*!

(Hallmark, I ain't!)

Next year-

Like people who live in Missouri,
"Show me" or there could be fury!
Now we ain't Christmas carol'n
We're singin' birthday to Carolyn
Where she works in open heart recovery

(Ok, these past few years I've used up all the words I can find that rhyme with Carolyn and Faber, so don't expect much next year. Till then, happy birthday!)

ELLIOT

Happy birthday, Elliot,
Whatever I'm buying you'd selliot…
But your political agenda
Could at times use some Splenda—
And some words that you use I can't quite spelliot!

(My apologies to Nipsey Russell)

ELLEN

On this milestone birthday—you get rhymes with fifty,
Or thrifty, or swifty, or "you're just so nifty."
But those are cute and yeah—they are true…
But it just won't encompass all that is you

So much of your time
Raising Franny and Jenny
Marc, too, puts in days
(But maybe not as many)

For you are a mom
And to Marc, his bride
And those you call friends
We treasure with pride

But fifty's just a number
That we think too much of…
So if we just think of Ellen
Then we all think of love!

Happy and healthy birthday!

("*All You Need Is Love*" was already taken by the Beatles)

HAPPY BIRTHDAY RON, "MOOSE" KING!

If you give a moose a muffin
If you give a moose a beer
Would he dance about and sing aloud!
Would he toast to all "good cheer"?

If you give a moose a pizza
Would he smile and know that all!
That all of us, right here today,
Wish him a wonderful birthday ball!

HAPPY BIRTHDAY RUSSELL YOUNG

It's birthday time for Russell Young
He loves life's cheapest pleasures…
No fax, computer, or cellular phone—
No runs, no hits, no errors

But time has changed
He's no more in neutrality
Russell has a cellular phone—
Welcome to reality!

The beeps, the buzzes
The ring, and the text
Vibrate from your pocket
Not knowing what's next

So wired for sound
With wireless deluxe
He's not too happy
He screams, "This sucks!"

HAPPY BIRTHDAY

No rhyme this time
Well, maybe there is—
I just didn't want you to expect it,
But since it's your day
I'll go ahead anyway
So you won't have to feel neglected

Happy Birthday!

RUSTY

In April each year, it's baseball we cheer
For the boys of summer arrive…
But also, each year, when April is here
Another life seems to revive…

The sky may get dark, with a walk in the park
While the rain brings life to the musty…
But get on your mark as the sun will embark
And the *Young* will never get *Rusty*!

A BIRTHDAY SONG FOR DENNIS

"Number 8 ½" not to be confused with "Number 9"
(Sung to the tune of "Yellow Submarine," loosely, that is…)

In a town, where he was born, lived a man—who came to be…
As he stood beneath a sign—it read: "See me, to want to see."
So he gave an eye exam to one and all of us—who'd long to see…
So he'd ask, if better one, or better two—would be blurry…

We all knew Dennis—when he had long hair (*hair!*)
When he had long hair (*hair!*), when he had long hair (*hair!*)
We all knew Dennis—when he had long hair (*hair!*)
When he had long hair (*hair!*), when he had long hair (*hair!*)

And our friends, are gathered round,
And many more of them-are on the floor…
And we all, began to drink!

(*Loud consumption noise!*)

(We don't need patients anymore—We're slowing down…No, Dr. Cuervo
doesn't work on Friday! That's it, that's it—It's *happy hour!*)

As he lives his life of ease, with a Cuervo and cold Murine…
Where color blue (*color blue*), is sometimes green (*is sometimes green*)
Or cannot be defined—your color blind—*ah ha*—

We all knew Dennis—when he had long hair (*hair!*)
When he had long hair (*hair!*), when he had long hair (*hair!*)
We all knew Dennis—when he had long hair (*hair!*)
When he had long hair (*hair!*), when he had long hair (*hair!*)

CAROL

Happy birthday, Carol…
From me here on Facebook,
The years that you were dealt
Appear you never took!

If I hadn't known you long—
I certainly couldn't tell…
That, yes, in fact you took those years—
And certainly, hid them well…

Some say it's easy living,
And some—it's your cosmetics…
But I know your mom and sister, too
Which proves that it's genetics!

So here's a wish for your big day
"Your happiness and your health,"
But just in case you're hiding something—
I wish you'd spread the wealth!

Cheers!

HAPPY BIRTHDAY GREG AND BIG AL

It's the autumnal equinox
But that isn't all
Two birthdays abound
On this date I recall

Young James Gregory
I've known since I was six
You still have surprises
In your big bag of tricks

And, too, Big Al
One of my fine navy buds
We quaffed us a few
Of some rum and some suds

But this year's equinox
Falls on the twenty-third
So I hoist you a toast—
(Mine'll be shaken not stirred)

BIG AL "THE LEGEND"

The twenty-first of September
I still can remember
My ol' shipmates twenty-first birthday…

In P.I. we stumbled
And hearts they all tumbled
As Al traveled down Magsaysay.

A$$hole and elbows
To reap all he sows
That hot and tropical night…

Until that next morning
Without too much warning
He returned with a smile clear and bright!

A happy good time
He said right on time
At quarters that very next morn…

For when Liberty Call went down
We headed back on the town
And soon "the Legend" was born!

Happy birthday, Big Al!

JIM

I wish you a happy healing
And I know this isn't a joke...
But regardless of what your doc has said-
He sold you a joint you couldn't smoke!

(Hallmark ain't got nothing on me!)

ONE FOR MY AUNT

Happy Hanukkah—
Hear my rant...
About Aunt Flo'
My favorite "Ant!"

Always thoughtful
And full of class
With love for you
I raise my glass!

For that and for this
I thank you a lot...
When it comes to kindness
You're the sultan of swat!

Happy Hanukkah!

CHEER UP

Disguised inside this little verse
A note for your file...
Pull it out when you are down
'Cause I love it when you smile!

Just what's on this little note—
I am here to tell...
That if someone upsets your day—
Be sure and give 'em *hell*!

AKRUB GIRLS

Happy birthday to the "Akrub" Girls
Your exploits keep us amused
Plus—you ladies never looked so good
While some feel battered and bruised

But milestone birthdays took us over the hump…
Last year—it sure was fun…
Besides—they say fifty's the new forty these days
So to you two—happy forty-one!

MARY

It was forty years ago today,
Jackie got a little sister to play...
In a house in Kanawha City
Where they grew up so pretty
And made aging seem oh so passé

From that first case of beer
For your twenty-first year
My—you were so young and sporty
But now it's wine if there's time
While your still in your prime—
At least, until you reach forty!

RICK

So you're heading out west—
You'll make it the best,
I know that you're surely gonna…
'Cause with jobs galore
you can open a store—
By selling some prime marijuana!

But should you decide—
To take it in stride
You're a success wherever you roam…
'Cause it don't really matter
if your wallet gets fatter—
It's here that you'll always call home!

Safe and joyous travels

HAPPY BIRTHDAY TO YOU, AUNT FLO

I'm sorry that this is late
I wish you the best—as I always do
And hope that your day was great

But one great day is not good enough
You're deserving of so much more
There aren't enough words to describe all you're due
But know that it's you I adore!

A POEM FOR A MOTHER TO HER DAUGHTER

To my child
So full of wonder
A part of me
Is cast asunder

Think of me
As you spread your wings
And give to others
What your heart sings

Know of me
And of my soul
We're spread apart
And then made whole

TWO FRIENDS OF MINE

Two friends of mine are moving south
And I know not where to begin
To wish their future all the best
And forget not where they've been

For where they've been having left a mark
That we won't get rid of
A mark inside of all of us
Where all we have is love

To Greg, my friend, or should I say
My lifelong banded brother
If I had a choice to choose
I would not choose another

Through youthful days of growing up
Not all remembered exactly
But my favorite day was when I was away
And you found the lovely Jackie

So when I say that I don't know
Just where and how to begin
You just find a great big house
'Cause, I'll be movin' in!

POEMS FOR TERRI

(Because Jackie Made Me Write Them!)

Once I had this crush…
But in silence, I kept my hush
Then she gave her heart to Matt
And my dreams all went splat
Yet I still think of her and gush!

To write one whom I didn't marry
A poem seems somewhat contrary…
But I'll give it a shot—
'Cause I still find her hot
And my feelings I'll just have to bury!

The eyes I once longed for were blue
But my path to her wasn't quite true
So I picked my own battle
While she moved to Seattle
And bid her the sweetest adieu

A POEM FOR A FRIEND OF JACKIE'S

(Karen)

To my role model
Who taught me good habits
Of child-rearing and rearing me, too
You're my friend and role mother
And above you no other
I raise my glass to you

A toast to you
You're all I adore
From lessons, you taught me so well
I give you always my best
You're above all the rest
Here's your secret that I want to tell…

If seventy's the new sixty
And sixty's the new fifty
(The math will prove this sum…)
Then fifty's the new forty
(And too because you're so sporty)
Then forty's the new thirty-one!

Any way you play it
I may as well say it—
(And thusly I hope and I pray…)
To send you good wishes
And hope all's delicious
On this, your thirty-first birthday!

Happy birthday!

FOR MY FRIEND, JO...

(Joanne Donated a Kidney to Honor the Memory of her Dearest Friend, Dawn)

No poem I'd write
Would serve you so right
For the wonderful deed that you've done
But I needed a ditty
That's not very witty
For doing what most of us shun

For the gift, you are giving
To help out the living
To honor the memory of dear, sweet Dawn...
So may the birds by your door
Acknowledge your chore
And sing you their sweetest song

FOR MY FRIEND AMANDA

(To Give to Her Daughter)

Child of my heart
You're so wonderful and smart
You light up my life like the sky

You're my joy and my pride
And you make me glass-eyed
When adversity you can defy

I will always be here
Whether you're far-off or near
Even when I'm not to be seen

'Cause I love you, my dear
And I want that quite clear
Happy birthday, sweet sixteen!

GEORGE THE DOG

Nothing so lovely and so vibrant
As a journey to the fire hydrant,
Through the woods, another lap
And back again to take a crap

A THANK-YOU FOR MY BIRTHDAY!

A wonderful day
With friends was had
Your friendship was certainly the key
From Facebook posts
To cards and notes
It was a happy birthday for me!

Thank you, everyone!

BIRTHDAY FOR DIANA L.

Before dear Jackie and sweet little Mary
The legend, it told of another...
The winds, they blew cold
And thunder, it rolled...
But it wasn't for Louie, their brother

Still there's amiss
For the other big sis
Her whereabouts not quite unknown
But to set things straight
There's no time to wait
There's more that needs to be shown

At the Sterling, a-grillin'
Papa Jack was just chillin'
And all was just fine and dandy...
'Cause still in the mix
For a mom they all miss
And dearest of all, Sis Andi

But that thunder we heard
Was really absurd
And the wind really didn't blow cold...
Cause we all love to tease her
And we just wanna please her—
But want the whole truth to be told

So as I continue to say
I've been led astray

And I can't seem to stop this verse…
Our time spent with you
Is something we do
As a blessing for us, not a curse

So Diana I convey
A most happy birthday
Your presence is always worthwhile…
'Cause it's all been a sham
A farce and a scam
I just wanted to make you smile!

Happy birthday!

POEM—JIM

Happy birthday to you,
My dear ol' friend...
Here's to good times
And that they never should end

Seems milestone birthdays—
Are the trend for this year!
But time is irrelevant
With friends I hold dear

We had such a blast
Brought up in the East End...
Most rules weren't broken
Although some we'd just bend

I won't go into detail
'Bout the party and cops
But through the good and bad
I hope the fun never stops

Yes, we've seen quite a lot
Been through the thick and the thin!
And because of our friendship—
I'd do it all over again!

AUNT FLO'S NINETIETH

Through the years and through the tears
Of sorrow and jubilation

You always took the time for all
Forgoing all hesitation

Then one day you lit a spark
And Leon had no doubt

Though Detroit born and Detroit bred
You traveled the southerly route

He brought you here into our hearts
And here you made a home

Raising five in the *hood*
Where all of them would roam

But five is not just where you stopped
You welcomed more than that

To anyone upon your door
You'd spread a welcome mat

Your heart is larger than the rest
Which never did you flaunt

I'm blessed to be a part of your brood
And proud to call you Aunt

All that gather here today
Are proud to be a part

To celebrate the touching love
You've nestled in our heart

TO ALL THE MOTHERS

To all the mothers on my list whom I don't recognize
Here's a thought that's all for you—to clearly summarize
Just because you're not my mom doesn't mean that I don't care
From tiny children to adults
For what you all prepare—
I thank you for the laughs and tears
And all that you go through…
I thank you for the time you give when there's other things to do
There's just no way I can thank you all for each and every way
'Cause you deserve the love of all, and *happy mother's day!*

FATHER'S DAY

Today is a special day
Today is Fathers' Day
But to me it's not so special
For I think of you *every* day!

I think of silent lessons
Of which you would convey
I didn't always comprehend
Or remember even today

When we speak of our own purpose
And what it really means…
I often forget you had your own-
Journey, with your own dreams

So long ago, I was so young
That day in which you died…
And yet today is not alone
The only day I cried

I still seek out your counsel
From within and up above…
Still seeking unlearned lessons
You gave to me with love

So as today, like all the others
We're not so far apart…
For my everlasting love for you—
Remains inside my heart

Thanks, Dad!

IVOR'S POEM

Year in, year out—you sang about—
Those songs that others sang...
But I can recall (not famous at all)
Your King Sound recording gang

On vinyl 45—you kept it alive—
Any venue, you'd "Rock 'n' Roll"
But your Motown sound you had to lay down...
With the Interpreters "You've Got Soul"

You touch us all with your "catter'n waul"
You get each of us out of our seats...
From fancy hotel halls or a place without walls—
You have us "Dancing in the Streets!"

From basement to dignitary—all calls, each inquiry
You'd even travel to the coast...
But here at home, you're never alone—
Cause it's "home" that loves you the most!

HAPPY BIRTHDAY, HARRY

Here's to your birthday, Harry Bell
And your prescription for staying well…
It's the "D-man" that you're embracin'
With Carrie inciting your heart a racin'
And her conducting it faster than the *William Tell*!

DIANA

To Diana, a little verse
A rhyme, which I had not...
To place upon your Facebook page—
As if I had forgot

A happy day I wish you had
Not limited to one day...
But more wonders and joys bestow
Far after your birthday

To those whom are blind
Can't see just how kind
The years have been to you...
For each year they hide
What's thought far and wide
That age may put yourself through

But each day we see
As with eyes on the sea
The beauty beside that cabana
Which you stand beside
As the years bow and abide
And send birthday wishes to Diana!

THANK YOU

Thank you, Janey! For the concert tickets
Only one thing I found was contrary...
The music was *great*
But instead of a date
I got stuck with my cousin Gary!

You're rhyming chops have much potential
While weekend's forecast is rain torrential
Stay inside and watch the 'eers
And thanks again as I say *cheers*!

WISHES FOR GREG

Five decades and more
To ol' James Gregory…
Birthday wishes—
With on top, a cherry

As always, the best,
As my brother and friend
Knowing the future
Hasn't an end

So glasses be raised
A toast without veto—
And just like Key West—
With a mango mojito

Happy birthday, Dr. Sunshine

GARY

It was long ago—fifty years today
I found a new friend up the street to play

Living it up—there in the East End
Then came Greg and Jim, we'd soon befriend

Fifty long years—some stories are rare
And since we're not in Vegas—I'm gonna share...

Record snowfall gave us snow days from school...
We'd shovel our walks then play basketball at *shul*

Without cash in our pockets, we'd go to his house to eat
Back then we didn't twitter and we certainly didn't tweet!

With Flo at the Diamond, where she worked way back then
So us four boys by ourselves we would fend

Gary would brag just how he could cook
So we just smiled, and a step back we all took

Now Gary impressed as the culinary king
Until he asked, "Where's that turner-over thing?"

Year's before, in New York as a kid
Ivor told stories of what his little brother did

Once at Ilene's, with an intruder at the door
But with Ivor's quick thinking, the guy was done for!

He threatened to cut him, to end the man's life
Till he saw Gary retrieved him a small butter knife

Back home playing ball, in the street or sandlot
Gary announced to us all, "Hey, guys—guess what?"

He told such tall stories, and some smelled with a stench
And said, "I got catcher's mask worn better than Johnny Bench!"

Years later in a bar, becoming of age
Well, maybe they weren't but were willing to engage

They didn't think they'd get quite this far
But were just proud of themselves to be in a bar

Happy they made it—and the waitress wasn't pushy
But then Gary chimed, "I want something *slushy*"

Times were different—in this town we call home…
Today he'd be tossed, when their cover was blown

Now Morgantown bound, and through life's twists and turns
We'd discover so much, and much we would learn

Like when Ivor could sing an "*Old Blue Eyes*" tune
We learned *never* to ask Gary to sing Frampton's "*I'm in You*"

He'd lay in his bed with headphones on his head
And he'd scream out this song—that could wake up the dead!

But now we're much calmer————we're all more content
Then we go on a "guys trip" and hope what breaks just only gets bent!

Like at football games to Blacksburg—he made us all laugh
When he approached the cops—the VA Tech staff

But all was okay, all was in order
Hell, we didn't even miss him—until the fourth quarter!

But remember Johnny Bench, and that great catcher's mask?
Gary lost the booze from an FBI's agent's flask

So there you all have it—just to make you all aware
Of just some of the adventures of our beloved Gary....
Happy birthday!

JANE'S LAW

On a milestone birthday you get "rhymes with fifty."
Like thrifty or swifty or "you're just so nifty."
But those are cute and yeah—they are true…
But it just won't encompass—all that is you
So let me expound, but just a wee bit
So all that don't know, won't be quick to acquit.

You're a great mom to Dirk, but Seamus ain't talking…
Cindy likes Dad, while Dirk keeps squawking
You make your house a home, and you take care of Jim
He dedicates to you, his heart, soul, and limb
All here attest to your wit, wisdom, and charm
And any courtroom aggressor, you emphatically disarm.

So now all here should know, that with each *bark, meow, and caw,*
What this document proclaims, now is *Jane's law!*

THE FINAL SUBJECT

Feel good!

If you don't…look at yourself in the mirror and *smile*!
Smile until you "feel" your smile and accept the joy that is
rightfully yours. It *is* yours!
Be grateful and *smile*!
Feel the joy…now *stay* there!
Just smile!

If you read no other rhymes or rants in this collection,
please read this one and try it. My only goal is for you to
feel good. Feel good about yourself, your surroundings,
your friends, your work…and be grateful.
Be as grateful as I am grateful to you for having this in your
possession.

Thank you! *Thank you very much!*

Close your eyes. Fall in love—stay there.
—Rumi

Made in the USA
Lexington, KY
20 April 2018